SOUND

The Wit of the

BEATLES

BITES

SOUND

The Wit of the

BEATLES

BITES

Michael O'Mara Books Limited

First published in Great Britain in 2005 by
Michael O'Mara Books Limited
9 Lion Yard
Tremadoc Road
London SW4 7NQ

A CIP catalogue record for this book is available from the British Library

ISBN 1-84317-153-8

3 5 7 9 10 8 6 4 2

Compiled by Helen Cumberbatch
Picture research by Judith Palmer
Designed and typeset by Design 23

Printed and bound in Singapore by Tien Wah Press

Introduction

Initially formed as a skiffle band known as the Quarry Men in the late 1950s, the Beatles finally emerged in 1960 as a fledgling rock'n'roll outfit, and by January 1962 they had engaged the services of a manager, Brian Epstein. Five months later, the boys had signed their first record deal with EMI Records' Parlophone label, run by George Martin.

As word of their energetic rock'n'roll performances, sublimely catchy records, and unparalled charisma began to spread, it wasn't long before John, Paul, George and Ringo were taking Britain, and indeed the rest of the world, by storm. On tours throughout the world an outbreak of Beatlemania was guaranteed wherever the band was playing. Indeed it was while they were on their travels that the Beatles' cheeky wit was most keenly evident. When faced with a barrage of oft-repeated questions from members of the world's press, the four young men would often amuse themselves by offering up a wide range of witty ripostes to a raft of less than intelligent enquiries, with tongue firmly in cheek.

In addition to chronicling engaging examples of droll banter from press conferences across the globe, *Sound Bites: The Wit of the Beatles* has also recorded the Beatles' entertaining exchanges with, among others, their manager and record-label boss, as well as recounting mirthful moments from various live events, thereby capturing the essence of the Fab Four's uniquely hilarious humour.

Early Days – Banter With Brian

In November 1961, when music-shop owner Brian Epstein first saw and heard the Beatles live in Liverpool's Cavern Club, he was struck both by their music and their earthy, raw style. He decided to approach them to discuss the possibility of his becoming their manager and, after a few meetings, an agreement was eventually made in mid-December 1961.

The second business meeting the Beatles had with Brian Epstein on 6 December 1961 didn't get off to a good start. Though John, George, and original drummer Pete Best had arrived on time, Paul was still nowhere to be seen.

After half an hour Epstein began to get a little angry, and told George to give Paul a call. On being told that Paul had only just got out of bed and was having a bath, Epstein remarked in anger, 'How can he be late for such an important meeting?' George replied nonchalantly, 'Well, he's late, but he's very clean!'

Early Days – Joking With George

After the Beatles were turned down by Decca Records, George Martin, director of EMI's Parlophone label, gave them an audition. Martin could see the boys had tremendous potential, and so it was in June 1962 that the band signed their first recording contract.

On 4 September 1962, the Beatles began recording 'Love Me Do' at Abbey Road Studios in London, under producer George Martin's careful supervision. As Martin was anxious for the band members to understand the techniques used in the recording studio, and appreciate what was expected of them in the future, he spoke to them at length, before asking them if they had any questions.

No one said a word. The Beatles looked at one another with a mischievous glint in their eyes. Breaking the deathly silence, George Harrison simply remarked, 'Yeah, I don't like your tie!', a cheeky comment that was met with gales of laughter from the producer and his team.

Rattling Jewellery

On 4 November 1963, the Beatles played at the Royal Variety Performance at the Prince of Wales Theatre in London, in front of the Queen Mother, Princess Margaret (pictured meeting the Beatles after the show) and Lord Snowdon.

After singing three songs – 'From Me To You', 'She Loves You' and 'Till There Was You' – and engaging in some cheeky banter, John Lennon went on to introduce the final song, 'Twist and Shout', in uniquely memorable fashion: 'For our last number I'd like to ask your help. Would the people in the cheaper seats clap your hands? And the rest of you, if you'll just rattle your jewellery!'

Rapturous laughter followed, and the last Beatles number was played.

Make 'Em Laugh

On 2 December 1963, the Beatles appeared as guest artistes on the popular British comedy programme *The Morecambe and Wise Show*, which was recorded in front of a live studio audience. After first performing 'This Boy', 'All My Loving' and 'I Want To Hold Your Hand', the boys then agreed to collaborate with comedians Eric Morecambe and Ernie Wise on a special musical number, which was standard practice for all performers who were invited on the show.

The Beatles were willing participants in the self-mocking comedy skit, in which Eric Morecambe insisted on referring to Ringo as 'Bongo' and the whole band as 'the Kaye Sisters', a popular singing trio from the 1950s. The boys readily entered into the spirit of the show, and had George Harrison parodying the oft-mentioned reference to Ernie Wise's 'short, fat, hairy legs', by comically describing the Beatles as 'the ones with the big, fat, hairy heads', to howls of laughter from the others.

Dressed in garish, stripy, pink, white and blue jackets and matching boaters for their rendition of 'On Moonlight Bay', the Fab Four also had to contend with Eric Morecambe, clad in a collarless Beatles jacket and wearing a moptop wig, repeatedly singing 'twist and shout' and 'yeah yeah yeah' over the top of the melodic ballad. Not to be outdone, the Beatles ended the song with their trademark 'oooooh', thus proving that they were natural comedians and thoroughly prepared to hold themselves up to ridicule in the name of entertainment.

Moptop Madness

When the Beatles first arrived in the United States their hairstyle became the focus of intense media attention. In fact it was in the US that the term 'moptop' was first used, deriving from a report in the New York Herald Tribune, which revealed the hair-do to be a 'mop effect that covers the forehead, some of the ears and most of the back of the neck'. As a result, the Fab Four faced relentless questioning about their hair whenever they were on tour.

REPORTER: How do you feel about teenagers imitating you with Beatle wigs?
JOHN: *They're not imitating us because we don't wear Beatle wigs.*

REPORTER: What do you call that hairstyle you're wearing?
GEORGE: *Arthur.*

REPORTER: Can you ever go anywhere unnoticed?
PAUL: *When we take off our wigs . . .*

REPORTER: Some of your detractors allege that you are bald and those haircuts are wigs. Is that true?

JOHN: *We're all bald. And deaf and dumb too.*

REPORTER: Do you ever think of getting a haircut?

GEORGE: *No, love. Do you?*

REPORTER: Where'd you get the idea for your haircuts?

JOHN: *Where'd you get the idea for yours?*

REPORTER: Do you ever get haircuts?

GEORGE: *I had one yesterday.*

RINGO: *That's no lie.*

GEORGE: *Honest, that's the truth!*

REPORTER: I think he missed!

RINGO: *You should have seen him the day before!*

REPORTER: Do you wear wigs?
JOHN: *If we do they must be the only ones with real dandruff!*

REPORTER: Where do your hair-dos originate from?
GEORGE: *Our scalps.*

REPORTER: Where did you get your hairstyle?
PAUL: *From Napoleon. And Julius Caesar too. We cut it any time we feel like it.*
RINGO: *We may do it now!*

REPORTER: How can you sleep at night with your hair so long?
JOHN: *Well, when you're asleep at night you don't notice!*

REPORTER: What excuse do you have for your collar-length hair?
JOHN: *Well, it just grows out yer head.*

REPORTER: What's the biggest threat to your careers: the atom bomb or dandruff?
RINGO: *The atom bomb. We've already got dandruff.*

REPORTER: Does your hair require any special attention?
JOHN: *Inattention is the main thing.*

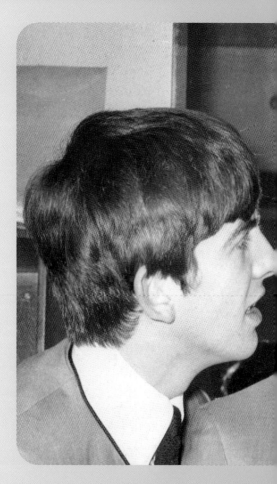

More Japes With George

In January 1964 the Beatles were in France for a show at the Olympia in Paris. During their stay in the city they were scheduled to record German versions of 'I Want To Hold Your Hand' and 'She Loves You', but on the day they were due in the studio the boys were nowhere to be seen.

George Martin waited for an hour before ringing their hotel, and was informed by their assistant, Neil Aspinall, that the boys had told him to tell the producer that they weren't coming… Martin decided to go to the hotel himself to find out what was going on, but when he arrived at their suite in the George V hotel, he discovered that they were having what looked like a Mad Hatter's tea party in the middle of the room. His unexpected entrance provoked a flurry of slapstick activity. 'They exploded in all directions. They ran behind couches, and one put a lampshade on his head to hide! They just did Goon things, and a chorus of "Sorry, George. Sorry, George," came from behind the sofa!' as George Martin recalled.

He didn't stay angry with them for long, however, and they were eventually persuaded to return to the studio and do the German recordings as intended.

The Beatles Abroad

On 7 February 1964, the four members of the Beatles, along with George Martin and Brian Epstein, flew to the US together for the first time. When they arrived at John F. Kennedy airport in New York, the band attended a press conference, in which they responded to their many questioners with snappy replies, wisecracks and ad-libs. In a later interview, George Harrison remarked, 'They started asking us funny questions, so we just started answering them with stupid answers.' It was a routine they would find themselves repeating at every press conference throughout the world.

REPORTER: How did you find America?
RINGO: *We went to Greenland and made a left turn.*

REPORTER: Have you heard about the 'Stamp out the Beatles' campaign in Detroit?
PAUL: *First off, we're bringing out the 'Stamp out Detroit' campaign!*

REPORTER: What do you expect to find here in Australia?
JOHN: *Australians, I should think!*

During a press conference in San Francisco in August 1964, Ringo Starr was quizzed about the 'Ringo for President' campaign that had begun during the Beatles' summer trip to the States. All the Beatles were in full support of it. 'We think he should win. Definitely in favour,' said John Lennon.

REPORTER: Would you make them [the Beatles] part of your cabinet?
RINGO: *I'd have to, wouldn't I?*
GEORGE: *I could be the door.*
JOHN: *I could be the cupboard.*

REPORTER: How come you were turned back by Immigration?
JOHN: *We had to be deloused.*

REPORTER: The French haven't made up their minds about the Beatles. What do you think of them?
JOHN: *Oh, we like the Beatles!*

REPORTER: Do you speak French?
PAUL: *Non.*

REPORTER: You and the snow came to Washington today. Which do you think will have the greater impact?
JOHN: *The snow will probably last longer.*

REPORTER: What do you do when you're cooped up in a hotel room between shows?
GEORGE: We *ice skate*.

As the Beatles cruised off the coast of Miami Beach on a 93-foot luxury yacht *Southern Trail*, Ringo commented, 'It's hotter than it is at Blackpool on an August Bank Holiday!'

REPORTER: You Beatles have conquered five continents. What would you like to do next?
THE BEATLES (in unison): *Conquer six!*

REPORTER: Do you ever get homesick when on a long tour like this?
JOHN: *Oh, yeah, you get homesick all right ... But we have a great and wild time, and look at all these gifts [we get]. Some of them are really unusual. The other day I got a bra with 'I Love John' embroidered across it. I didn't keep it, though, because it really didn't fit!*

During a television interview following the Washington DC concert in 1964, the presenter had to contend with a rather lively John Lennon ...

REPORTER: Which one are you?
JOHN: *I'm Eric.*
REPORTER [pointing toward the TV camera]: Eric, here is the American public.
JOHN: *I'm John. It's only a joke.*
REPORTER: Yes, well, John ... here is the American public. These are the forty million American viewers ...
JOHN: *It only looks like one man to me ... Oh, it's the cameraman!*

Heartfelt Humour

In March 1964 the Beatles attended the Variety Club of Great Britain's prize-giving ceremony to receive the Show Business Personalities of 1963 award. After Harold Wilson (the Leader of the Opposition) had presented the boys with their Silver Heart trophies, John made his acceptance speech.

'Thanks for the Purple Hearts,' he quipped, referring to a US military medal awarded to soldiers wounded in action, which provoked much amusement in the audience.

'Silver! Silver!' Ringo shouted out, correcting his fellow Beatle.

'Oh, yes. Sorry about that, Harold!' John replied, in mock apology.

When George accepted his award at the same event he remarked: 'It's very nice indeed to get . . . especially to get one each because we usually have a bit of trouble cutting them in fourths!'

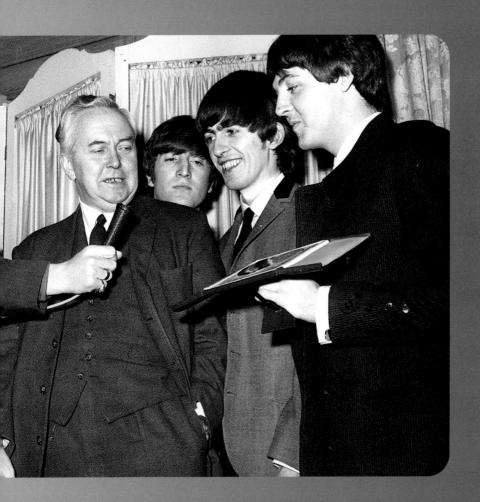

Beatles on Film

In March 1964, during the filming of *A Hard Day's Night*, the Beatles' first movie, there was always much hilarity on set as the boys enjoyed their first foray in the world of film. They were actively encouraged to express themselves as freely as possible, though not every scene made it to the final cut. According to their co-actor Victor Spinetti, the Beatles wouldn't always follow the script, and were unpredictable in their madcap behaviour: 'You never knew what they were going to say or do. They had to cut so many scenes. Honestly, if you could get all of the outtakes, you'd have another film... They sent each other up all the time. They'd say things like, "Paul, you're the prettiest. You get out of the car first." As the lunatic director, I'd walk up to them and say, "You're late. You should have been at rehearsals ages ago." John would say, "You're not a television director. You're Victor Spinetti acting as a television director!"'

REPORTER: Can we look forward to any more Beatles movies?
JOHN: *Well, there'll be many more, but I don't know whether you can look forward to them or not!*

PAUL: *There was a scene where I'm supposed to be picking on Ringo and saying, 'It's all your fault.' And as I was saying it, I kept flapping my arms up and down . . . I don't know why . . . And he couldn't stand it . . . he was giggling away. So then I started laughing and we just collapsed. We did so many takes of it.*

RINGO: *Twelve takes on that one.*

PAUL: *. . . and they cut the bit in the end.*

REPORTER: What's your favourite part of the film?

JOHN: *All of us liked the bit in the field where we all jump about like lunatics because that's pure film, as the director told us . . . and we could've been anybody, but we enjoyed it.*

REPORTER: Are you going to have a leading lady in the film you're about to make?

PAUL: *We're trying to get the Queen. She sells in England, you know.*

REPORTER: When are you starting your next movie?

PAUL: *In February.*

GEORGE: *We have no title for it yet.*

RINGO: *We have no story for it yet.*

JOHN: *We have no actors for it yet.*

Money (That's What I Want)

The Beatles were often asked questions about their wealth and earnings, particularly while touring in the US, and in response would always reply with typical cheek and wit.

REPORTER: John, are you a millionaire?
JOHN: *No! That's another lousy rumour. Wish it were true!*
REPORTER: Well, then, where does all the money go?
JOHN: *Well, a lot of it goes to Her Majesty.*
GEORGE: *She's a millionaire!*

REPORTER: What will you do when Beatlemania subsides?
JOHN: *Count the money.*

REPORTER: Will you sing a song for us?
JOHN: *No. Sorry, we need money first.*

However, the subject of money was an important issue to the four young men from Merseyside, despite the jokes they made about it.

REPORTER: How do you add up success?
THE BEATLES (all together): *Money!*

REPORTER: What do you do with all your money?
RINGO: *We bury it.*
GEORGE: *We hide it.*
PAUL: *We don't see it. It goes to our office.*

Somebody said to me, 'But the Beatles were anti-materialistic.'
That's a huge myth. John and I literally used to sit down and say,
'Now, let's write a swimming pool.'
Paul McCartney

Taxmen

The fact that so much of their earnings was lost to the Inland Revenue made the issue of tax a sore point as far as the Beatles were concerned.

REPORTER: How much money do you expect
to make here [in New York]?
JOHN: *About half a crown. Depends on the tax. How much have you got?*

REPORTER: One of you said you didn't like politics. What about in your
own country? You're going back to a general election campaign.
JOHN: *If we can find out which one takes the least tax I'll vote for them.*

REPORTER: What do you do with all your money?
JOHN: *We pay a lot of taxes.*

Beatlemania

Despite the madness surrounding the phenomenon of Beatlemania, the Fab Four managed to keep their sanity in the face of relentless press interest.

REPORTER: Do you believe in lunacy?
RINGO: *Yeah, it's healthy!*
REPORTER: But aren't you embarrassed by all the lunacy?
RINGO: *No, it's crazy!*

REPORTER: What's your reaction to a Seattle psychiatrist's opinion that you are a menace?
GEORGE: *Psychiatrists are a menace.*

REPORTER: How do you keep your psychic balance?
RINGO: *The important thing is not to get potty. There's four of us so, whenever one of us gets a little potty the other three bring him back to earth.*

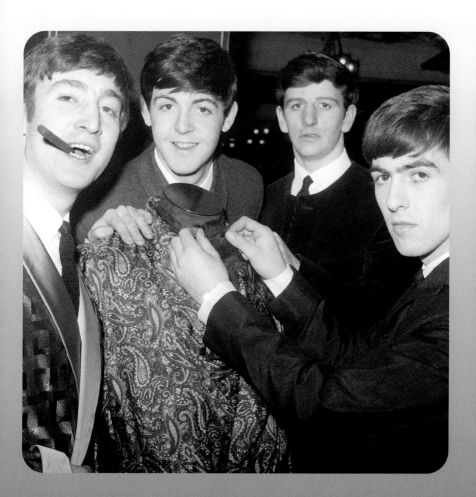

Musical Insights

The origins of the Beatles' lyrics and the true meaning behind their many songs were often the focus of intense speculation by the fans and especially by the media. Consequently, the Beatles were regularly asked bizarre questions about their music, to which they would reply with typically droll (or sometimes equally bizarre) responses, particularly to questions of a more obscure nature.

REPORTER: What do you think you've contributed to the musical field?
RINGO: *Records.*

REPORTER: A recent article in *Time* magazine put down pop music, and referred to 'Day Tripper' as being about a prostitute and 'Norwegian Wood' about a lesbian. I want to know what your intent was when you wrote them.
PAUL: *We were just trying to write songs about prostitutes and lesbians!*

REPORTER: About the song 'Eleanor Rigby', what was the motivation for that?
JOHN: *Two queers!*

Girls, Girls, Girls

The private lives of the Beatles and their interest in women were popular subjects for the world's press, and so the four young men were constantly quizzed about both their own personal relationships and their general views on the opposite sex.

REPORTER: What kind of girls do you prefer?
RINGO: *My wife.*
REPORTER: What kind of girl is she?
RINGO: *A nice girl.*
REPORTER: What kind of girl do you like, Paul.
PAUL: *John's wife!*

REPORTER: Will Paul tell us a little bit about his marriage plans?
PAUL: *You've just asked me. The thing is, you see, everyone keeps saying I'm married or I'm divorced or I've got fifty children, but I haven't ...*
RINGO: *You've only got forty!*

REPORTER: One of your countrymen said on his arrival in England that he thought American women were out of style for not wearing mini-skirts and as they didn't wear them their legs were ugly.
RINGO: *Well, if they don't wear mini-skirts, how does he know their legs are ugly?!*

REPORTER: With all these girls chasing you all over the world, who's the most exciting woman you've ever met?
JOHN: *Ringo's mother was pretty hot! I'm only joking . . .*

REPORTER: Ringo, in California the girls ate some grass you walked on. How do you feel about that?
RINGO: *I just hope they don't get indigestion.*

REPORTER: Would you ever accept a girl in your group if she could sing, play an instrument and wear the Beatle haircut?
RINGO: *How tall is she?*

REPORTER: What do you think of the rumours that get spread about you in gossip magazines?
JOHN: *I don't give it much thought ... other than the one about my wife having more children than I can account for!*

When George Harrison was spotted taking out a mystery woman to dinner in London in 1963, he faced inevitable questioning about her identity. His evasively witty reply was: 'Her name is Hush-Hush and she's a friend of the family. As you'll probably guess from her name, she's Chinese!'

Fantastic Fans

When the Beatles played in public during their heyday in the 1960s, their performances were usually drowned out by the shouts and screams made by hundreds of hysterical female fans, to the extent that their music could barely be heard over the noise from the crowd. It was a situation that the foursome soon got used to; indeed it was something that seemed to bother the press more than the Beatles themselves.

REPORTER: Paul, why do teenagers scream when the Beatles appear?
PAUL: *None of us know. We kind of like the screaming teenagers. If they want to sit out there and shout, that's their business . . . The commotion doesn't bother us any more. It's like working in a bell factory. After a while you get used to the bells!*

REPORTER: Does all the adulation from teenage girls affect you?
JOHN: *When I feel my head start to swell, I look at Ringo and know perfectly well we're not supermen.*

The issue of safety was of paramount importance when the Beatles were being transported from gig to gig, no matter where they were in the world. Consequently, in collaboration with local police and promoters, their management kept having to think up more elaborate means of disguise than ever before. In Birmingham, for example, the police came up with 'Operation Beat-the-Beatlemania', in which the band got dressed up in policemen's overcoats and constables' helmets. In Doncaster the boys donned old macs and were driven around in an old yellow news van, while down the road in Sheffield the Beatles combed their hair into choirboys' quiffs to avoid being recognized.

REPORTER: There are ten thousand people in this auditorium [Wembley Arena] right now. There must be another ten thousand outside. We came in with George Harrison's mother, and there were so many people who recognized her and were banging on her car. Doesn't this bother you after a while?

RINGO: *Well, it doesn't bother me if they bang on Mrs Harrison's car . . . !*

REPORTER: Do you resent fans ripping up your sheets for souvenirs?

RINGO: *No, I don't mind. So long as I'm not in them while the ripping is going on.*

The effects of the madness surrounding Beatlemania led one promoter to suggest that it wouldn't be long before 'the Beatles will have to be brought into a hall in a cage, perform in a cage and leave in a cage!' This prediction was almost realized at a special fan-club show in Wimbledon in December 1963. The Fab Four found themselves performing on a makeshift platform that was enclosed behind a large steel mesh. In spite of the barrier, however, the fans still tried hard to get close to the group. Making light of the unusual situation, John Lennon remarked, 'If they press any harder they'll come through as chips!'

REPORTER: What would you do if the fans got past the police lines?
GEORGE: *We'd die laughing!*

Award-Winning Beatles

In June 1965 the Beatles were notified by Buckingham Palace that each of them had been awarded Membership of the Most Excellent Order of the British Empire (MBE) in the Queen's Birthday Honours List, the recommendation having been made by Prime Minister Harold Wilson.

REPORTER: Ringo, how do you feel about going to the Palace in your morning suit?

RINGO: *I don't mind. It'll be all right, when I buy one.*

REPORTER: You haven't got one then?

RINGO: *No, not yet. I've got an evening suit. If that will do.*

REPORTER: Oh, I don't think it will.

RINGO: *Well then, I'll just go in me pyjamas.*

During the ceremony in October 1965, Queen Elizabeth II asked the Beatles some probing questions.

HER MAJESTY: How long have you been together now?

PAUL: *Oh, for many years.*

RINGO: *Forty years!*

HER MAJESTY [addressing Ringo]: Are you the one who started it?

RINGO: *No, I was the last to join. I'm the little fellow.*

HER MAJESTY [addressing John]: Have you been working hard lately?

JOHN: *No, we've been on a holiday.*

News of the Beatles' MBEs provoked an outcry in the British media, and hundreds of letters were sent to the Palace from across the country, resolutely opposing the bestowal of such an award.

Many war veterans and politicians spoke out against the nomination, and indeed some former recipients of royal awards even sent back their medals in disgust. Among them were the French Canadian MP Hector Dupuis, who returned his MBE insignia, declaring that he did not wish to be 'a member of an Order which recognizes stupidity and hysteria'. In response, George Harrison declared, 'If Dupuis doesn't want the medal, he had better give it to us. Then we can give it to our manager, Brian Epstein. MBE really stands for "Mr Brian Epstein"!'

Despite the opposition to their receiving the MBE, the Beatles remained upbeat.

RINGO: *It's a good idea that younger people are getting the MBE now. Before, you got it when you were practically dead!*
GEORGE: *I think I'll take my medal down the antique shop to see what it's made of!*

Meeting the Maharishi

In summer 1967 the Beatles began a new spiritual journey under the guidance of the Maharishi Makesh Yogi. The relationship proved to be short-lived, however, after the band members became disillusioned with their guru's true motives, so after a period of time spent on retreat in India, the Beatles came home, with Ringo describing the course as 'just like Butlins, on the Ganges'. Each was confronted by journalists on their return, and deflected their questions with typical dry wit.

REPORTER: One Indian MP accused this place [the Maharishi's home] of being an espionage centre, and you, in fact, of being a spy for the West. Well, what happened?
PAUL: *Don't tell anyone. It's true. We're spies, yes. The four of us have been spies! Actually I'm a reporter and I joined the Beatles for that very reason, but the story's out next week in a paper that will be nameless.*

REPORTER: John, do you think the Maharishi is on the level?
JOHN: *I don't know what level he's on.*

Ringo's Ripostes

REPORTER: Do you like topless bathing suits?
RINGO: *We've been wearing them for years!*

REPORTER: One of your hits is 'Roll Over, Beethoven'.
What do you think of Beethoven as a composer?
RINGO: *He's great. Especially his poems.*

REPORTER: Ringo, why do you get the most fan mail?
RINGO: *I don't know, perhaps it's because more people
write to me.*

To the wine waiter at the 21 Bar in New York City
RINGO: *Do you have any vintage Coca-Cola?!*

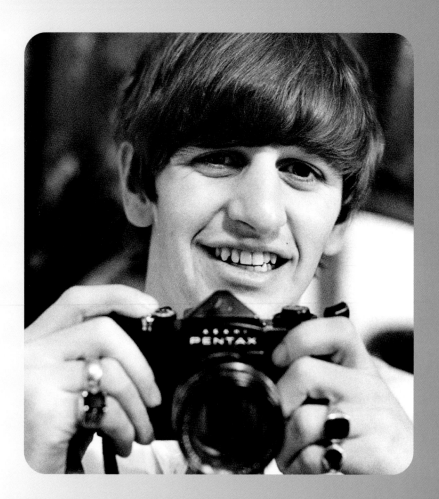

REPORTER: Ringo, why do you wear two rings on each finger?
RINGO: *Because I can't fit them through my nose!*

REPORTER: What started your practice of wearing four rings at once?
RINGO: *Six rings got to be too heavy.*

REPORTER: How tall are you?
RINGO: *Two feet, nine inches.*

REPORTER: Were you worried about the oversized roughnecks who tried
to infiltrate the airport crowd on your arrival?
RINGO: *That was us!*

Beatles on Beatles

In September 1963, during an interview with *Daily Mirror* journalist Donald Zec – who described the Beatles as 'cheeky-looking kids with Stone-Age hairstyles' – they were asked whether they were alike in any way. John replied: 'You know the way people begin to look like their dogs? Well, we're beginning to look like each other!'

REPORTER: What is it like being the Beatles?
GEORGE: *We've got to know each other quite well. We can stand each other better now than when we first met.*

REPORTER: Did you have a chance to get away from anybody at any time on the trip [their first to the US]?
GEORGE: *Yeah.*
RINGO: *He got away from me – twice!*

Beatles on Song

While the Beatles were touring in Adelaide, a reporter asked the band:
'Do you think you'll be writing any songs with Australian themes?'
John replied, 'No, we never write anything with themes. We just write the
same rubbish all the time.'

REPORTER: When you do a new song, how do you decide
who sings the lead?
JOHN: *We just get together and whoever knows most of the
words sings the lead.*

REPORTER: Do all the Beatles write songs?
JOHN: *Paul and I do most of the writing. George has written a few. Ringo hasn't
because it's hard to write something on the drums, isn't it?*
RINGO: *Yes!*

Miscellaneous Beatles Banter

REPORTER: Why don't you smile, George?
GEORGE: *I'll hurt my lips.*

While in New York in 1964, the Beatles received a tremendous reception from the fans. Such was the impact they had on the country, they even received support from notable American music idols, including Elvis Presley. On being told that Elvis had sent them a cable of congratulations, George Harrison asked cheekily, 'Elvis who?'

REPORTER: Do you have any special advice for teenagers?
JOHN: *Don't get pimples.*

REPORTER: The Vienna Boys' Choir is in town.
PAUL: *Ahhhh! We must go and see 'em! I've heard they're a rave!*
RINGO: *I believe they're wild, man. You gotta watch it when they're on.*
PAUL: *They blow up a bit of a storm, those fellas. Have you seen 'em shakin'-their-heads?*
RINGO: *I've seen 'em. Yeah.*
JOHN: *Vienna Boys' Choir Mania, I'd call it!*

REPORTER: Why do millions of Beatles fans buy millions of Beatles records?
JOHN: *If we knew, we'd form another group and become their managers.*

REPORTER: Do you enjoy press conferences?
JOHN: *Yes, depending on the intelligence of the questions.*

REPORTER: What do you think of the American girls as opposed to the British girls?
GEORGE: *They're the same, only they speak with an accent!*

REPORTER: Do you have nicknames you call each other?
JOHN: *I call George, Ray Coleman.*
GEORGE: *I call Ringo, Dave, but apart from that we don't.*
PAUL: *We're lying, of course.*

REPORTER: Paul, you lost your driver's licence, how did you do it?
PAUL: *I lost it a year ago . . . for speeding three times. If they catch you three times you lose it. [I] Got caught!*
RINGO: *He wasn't fast enough!*

REPORTER: Did any of you help Mr Epstein write his book [*A Cellarful of Noise*]?
JOHN: *No – he needed it though!*

REPORTER: You've admitted to being agnostics. Are you also irreverent?
PAUL: *We're agnostics, so there's no point in being irreverent!*

On arrival at JFK airport in February 1964, at the massive press conference where 200 members of the US media had gathered, one reporter asked: 'Do you come from a show-business background?'
'Well, me dad used to say me mother was a great performer!' said John.

REPORTER: Do you like Donald Duck?
RINGO: *No, I can't understand him.*
PAUL: *I can't either.*

FEMALE REPORTER: Do you date much?
RINGO: *What are you doing tonight?*

The End Is Nigh

One of the most oft-repeated questions in press conferences the world over concerned the Beatles' potential break-up. The four young men soon got used to inevitable speculation about their future together as a group, and would offer implausible replies to keep themselves amused.

REPORTER: What will you do when the bubble bursts?
GEORGE: *Take up ice hockey.*
PAUL: *Play basketball.*

REPORTER: What do you plan to do after the break-up of the Beatles?
PAUL: *No one's made any plans, but John and I will probably carry on songwriting, and George will go into basketball.*
GEORGE: *Or roller skating. I haven't really decided yet.*

Photograph Acknowledgements

Everett Collection/Rex Features 6–7;

Pictorialpress.com 8–9, 13, 28–9, 38, 42, 51;

PA/Empics 10–11, 34–5, 58;

IBL/Rex Features 15;

Keystone USA/Rex Features 16, 20–1, 23, 26-7, 46, 52, 56–7, 61, 62;

Tony Gale/pictorialpress.com 18–19, 32, 45, 72–3, 79;

Kevin Cole/Rex Features 24;

David Magnus/Rex Features 31, 76–7;

United Artists/pictorialpress.com 37;

J. Barry Peake/Rex Features 49;

Rex Features 64–5, 68–9, 71;

Sharok Hatami/Rex Features 66.